FEMININE & SUCCESSFUL

5 SIMPLE STEPS TO BECOME THE SUCCESSFUL WOMAN YOU ARE MEANT TO BE

INTRODUCTION

STEP 1:
EMBRACING YOUR LEADERSHIP IDENTITY

STEP 2:
BUILDING EMOTIONAL INTELLIGENCE

STEP 3:
DEVELOPING STRONG COMMUNICATION SKILLS

STEP 4:
NURTURING A SUPPORTIVE WORK ENVIRONMENT

STEP 5:
BALANCING CONFIDENCE AND HUMILITY

INTRODUCTION:

In today's rapidly evolving world, the concept of leadership has undergone a significant transformation. Among the emerging trends, feminine leadership stands out as a compelling and powerful approach that is gaining recognition and importance. The idea of feminine leadership goes beyond gender and embraces a set of qualities and characteristics associated with a more inclusive and empathetic style of leadership. As the year is 2023, it is evident from the available research that more women are rising into leadership roles at all levels, including elite executive positions, founders, CEOs, etc. Moreover, studies have shown that women possess certain advantages in leadership style.

The purpose of this ebook is to explore the significance of feminine leadership in today's world and provide valuable insights to aspiring female leaders and anyone interested in understanding this unique approach to leadership. In the pages that follow, you can expect to delve into the various aspects of feminine leadership, including its advantages, challenges, and strategies for success. We will draw from research and real-life experiences to shed light on the barriers women might face in leadership roles, such as prejudicial evaluations of their competence in masculine organizational contexts. Moreover, we will explore 5 steps through which women leaders can navigate these challenges and turn them into opportunities for personal and organizational growth.

This ebook aims to contribute to the development of successful feminine leaders by offering practical advice, actionable strategies, and inspiring stories from accomplished women in various fields. By examining the experiences of women who have broken barriers and achieved success, you will gain valuable insights into how feminine leadership can be a driving force for positive change and transformation. Moreover, the book emphasizes the significance of diverse leadership perspectives and how embracing feminine leadership can enrich and enhance the overall leadership landscape.

This ebook sets out to celebrate the contributions of women leaders, acknowledge the advantages of feminine leadership, and equip aspiring leaders with the tools and knowledge needed to succeed in their endeavors. By harnessing the power of feminine leadership, we believe individuals and organizations can foster a more inclusive, compassionate, and successful future.

LET'S ACTIVATE THE
DIVINE FEMININE

AND BECOME THE LEADER
WE ARE MEANT TO BE

STEP 1: EMBRACING YOUR LEADERSHIP IDENTITY

THE CONCEPT OF FEMININE LEADERSHIP

Feminine leadership is a leadership style characterized by traditionally feminine traits such as empathy, collaboration, emotional intelligence, and a holistic approach to decision-making. It prioritizes relationship-building, inclusiveness, and the well-being of team members. Feminine leaders listen to and empower their team, value diverse perspectives, and focus on long-term consequences of decisions. This leadership style benefits organizations by fostering teamwork, trust, and adaptability.
As women all the mentioned traits are inherently part of our essence, which is exactly what sets us up to be the successful leaders the world needs.

FINDING YOUR OWN LEADERSHIP STYLE

Embracing one's leadership identity and finding an authentic voice as a feminine leader is crucial for several reasons. Firstly, being true to oneself allows for genuine and sincere leadership, fostering trust and credibility among team members. Authenticity enables leaders to connect on a deeper level, enhancing communication and empathy. Secondly, embracing one's unique traits as a woman leader, such as empathy and intuition, can bring a fresh perspective to leadership and problem-solving.

By breaking free from societal expectations, women leaders can create a positive and inclusive work environment, encouraging collaboration and team effectiveness. Finally, being authentic allows women leaders to challenge gender stereotypes and inspire others to do the same, promoting diversity and gender equality in leadership positions.

HERE ARE FIVE QUESTIONS YOU CAN ANSWER THAT WILL HELP YOU FIND YOUR OWN LEADERSHIP STYLE

1. **What Motivates You as a Leader?** Reflect on the factors that inspire and motivate you to take on leadership roles. Consider the ways you connect with your team members and how you encourage them to excel.

2. **How Do You Handle Feedback?** Evaluate your receptiveness to feedback and your ability to use it to improve as a leader. Assess how you provide constructive feedback to your team members to help them grow and succeed.

3. What Communication Style Do You Use?

Understand your communication approach with team members and stakeholders. Identify whether you prefer a collaborative, democratic style or a more authoritative approach in decision-making.

4. How Do You Set and Maintain Accountability?

Examine how you establish clear expectations for your team and hold yourself and others accountable for meeting goals. Consider the methods you use to monitor progress and ensure productivity.

5. What Is Your Vision for Your Team or Organization?

Articulate your leadership vision and long-term goals for your team or organization. Clarify how your vision aligns with the overall mission and values of the company.

STEP 2:
BUILDING
EMOTIONAL
INTELLIGENCE

SIGNIFICANCE OF EMOTIONAL INTELLIGENCE

The significance of emotional intelligence in effective leadership cannot be overstated. Emotional intelligence enables leaders to build trust and rapport with their teams, communicate effectively, resolve conflicts, motivate and inspire employees, and adapt to change. It fosters a positive organizational culture, improves decision-making, and reduces employee turnover. Emotionally intelligent leaders create environments that promote collaboration, growth, and success, making it a vital skill for thriving in the dynamic and interconnected world of today's business landscape.

EMOTIONAL INTELLIGENCE CAN ENHANCE COMMUNICATION

Emotional intelligence, often denoted as EI or EQ, plays a pivotal role in enhancing communication, empathy, and decision-making skills in women. It involves recognizing and regulating emotions, both one's own and those of others. Women with strong emotional intelligence are adept at understanding non-verbal cues, enabling more effective communication. Empathy flourishes as they tune into others' emotions, fostering deeper connections.

In decision-making, emotional intelligence helps women consider feelings alongside logic, leading to well-rounded choices. Research shows EQ's significant impact on personal and professional success, transcending mere cognitive abilities.

DEVELOPING EMOTIONAL INTELLIGENCE (EI) FOR A SUPPORTIVE LEADERSHIP STYLE:

1. **Self-Awareness:** Recognize your emotions and their triggers. Regularly reflect on your feelings, thoughts, and reactions. This enhances understanding, leading to better self-regulation and empathetic responses to others' emotions.

2. **Active Listening:** Practice attentive listening to understand both spoken and unspoken feelings. This cultivates empathetic connections, fostering an inclusive and supportive environment for your team.

3. Conflict Resolution: Develop the skill to manage conflicts constructively. Utilize EI to remain composed, understand various perspectives, and guide discussions toward positive solutions, boosting team collaboration and trust.

STEP 3: DEVELOPING STRONG COMMUNICATION SKILLS

THE ROLE OF COMMUNICATION IN SUCCESSFUL LEADERSHIP

Effective leadership heavily relies on communication skills. The significance of adapting communication styles is something we want to highlight. Different styles can lead to misunderstandings, unclear priorities, and heightened stress. Furthermore, emotional intelligence is essential.
It's valued even more than technical skills by employers and aids in empathetic and influential leadership.

Communication plays a pivotal role in the successful execution of power.
Building relationships and connecting with the right people is crucial for leveraging power effectively.
Additionally, leadership traits and styles influence how communication is perceived and executed by leaders.
Effective leadership necessitates adapting communication styles, harnessing emotional intelligence, and skillfully utilizing power while maintaining meaningful relationships. These aspects collectively contribute to successful leadership that fosters collaboration, understanding, and achievement.

ACTIVE LISTENING, ASSERTIVENESS, AND NON-VERBAL CUES

Effective communication involves various elements like active listening, assertiveness, and non-verbal cues. Active listening entails techniques such as reflecting, asking open-ended questions, and paying attention to body language. Assertiveness, a vital aspect, helps express thoughts and needs while respecting others' opinions.

Effective non-verbal cues, including facial expressions and body language, complement verbal messages to convey emotions and intentions. These skills foster mutual understanding, empathy, and collaboration. Developing active listening skills is particularly valuable, aiding in relationship-building, problem-solving, and information retention.

STEP 4: NURTURING A SUPPORTIVE WORK ENVIRONMENT

THE IMPORTANCE OF CREATING AN INCLUSIVE AND SUPPORTIVE WORK ENVIRONMENT.

Creating an inclusive and supportive work environment is crucial for several reasons. It promotes respect for diverse backgrounds and encourages collaboration, which leads to a broader range of perspectives and ideas. An inclusive culture boosts employee satisfaction and retention, as individuals feel valued and are more likely to contribute innovative ideas without fear of judgment. Such an environment attracts top talent and enhances engagement, as employees have autonomy and feel comfortable expressing themselves.

An inclusive work environment is key to unlocking the full potential of both individuals and the organization as a whole.

Moreover, it fosters a sense of belonging and overall well-being, resulting in higher productivity and a positive company reputation.

HOW TO FOSTER AN INCLUSIVE CULTURE THAT EMPOWERS EVERYONE

Diversity brings varied perspectives and ideas, enhancing problem-solving and creativity. In an inclusive culture, all individuals feel valued, boosting employee satisfaction, retention, and innovation. To foster inclusivity:

1. Promote Open Communication: Encourage respectful dialogue where all voices are heard.
2. Provide Equal Opportunities: Ensure fair treatment and advancement for everyone.
3. Offer Diversity Training: Educate employees about biases and promote understanding.

4 TIPS FOR PROMOTING WORK-LIFE BALANCE AND SUPPORTING THE GROWTH AND DEVELOPMENT OF TEAM MEMBERS:

1. **Lead by Example:** Demonstrate healthy work-life balance practices yourself to set a positive tone and encourage your team to do the same.

2. **Flexible Work Arrangements:** Offer flexible schedules or remote work options to accommodate diverse needs and responsibilities.

3. Encourage Boundaries:

Support your team in setting clear boundaries between work and personal life. Encourage them to unplug after work hours and during vacations.

4. Clear Communication:

Set clear expectations, communicate project timelines, and encourage open conversations about workload to prevent burnout. Provide learning opportunities and growth paths aligned with individual career goals. Utilize feedback to tailor support and development strategies for each team member.

STEP 5: BALANCING CONFIDENCE AND HUMILITY

STEP 5: THE DELICATE BALANCE BETWEEN CONFIDENCE AND HUMILITY IN LEADERSHIP

Balancing confidence and humility in leadership is a nuanced art. Confident humility is a key concept, where leaders possess self-assuredness in their strengths while acknowledging their limitations. Striking this balance is essential as excessive confidence can lead to arrogance, while humility without confidence might hinder decision-making.

An effective leader acknowledges their expertise, yet remains open to learning and diverse perspectives. They admit mistakes and seek growth, fostering trust and approachability. This blend empowers leaders to make informed decisions, inspire teams, and create an environment that encourages collaboration and innovation.

CONFIDENCE AND HUMILITY AS A FEMININE LEADER

Combining confidence with humility allows feminine leaders to assert themselves while fostering collaboration, empathy, and growth within their teams and organizations. Remember, true leadership involves being authentic, open to growth, and responsive to the needs of those you lead.

Confidence Building:

- Embrace your strengths and accomplishments.
- Set clear goals and challenge yourself to learn new skills.
- Surround yourself with supportive mentors and peers.
- Practice positive self-talk and visualize success.

Humility Development:

- Listen actively to others and value their perspectives.
- Admit mistakes and learn from failures.
- Show appreciation for others' contributions.
- Continuously seek opportunities for self-improvement.

CONGRATULATIONS.
YOU MADE IT.

Dear Leaders,
As you embark on your journey with the ebook on feminine leadership, remember that knowledge is only valuable when applied. Embrace the insights gained from the book to create a leadership style that blends the strengths of both genders. Cultivate traits like discernment and humility, allowing you to judge well while staying open to new ideas. Champion participative and democratic approaches, appreciating the strengths of your team. Infuse your leadership with qualities that inspire collaboration, empathy, and sustainability. Remember that a balanced leadership style, drawing from both masculine and feminine traits, can pave the way for a just, kinder, and more inclusive future. Your commitment to evolving as a leader will not only uplift your team but also contribute to a positive impact on the world. We believe in you.
You are ready.
Best regards,
Yout team of
Art of All

ABOUT US:

WE SEE THE ART IN EVERYTHING.

Art of All is designed to celebrate and support the creativity and passion of multi-passionate individuals who have a diverse range of interests, talents, skills and passions and want to build a life including all of them.

At our Art of All Institute in Hamburg and in our Online Academy we provide creative workshops, business coachings, spiritual sessions, both 1:1 and in group sessions.
If you are interested in giving workshops in our Institute, please reach out!
We would love to hear from you.

Join us on our spiritual journey

FIND OUR NEXT OFFLINE DATES HERE:
www.theartofalloriginal.com